Pain: In Various Hues

The wave of pain and its Hues

Sarita Mishra

Made with ❤ on the BookLeaf Publishing Platform
www.bookleafpub.in
www.bookleafpub.com

Dedication

I owe you Bapa, Ma, and I have realised that many things said by you were true, but then it was your tone that bothered me......♥

I love you Bijoy, Naisha and Naima, thank you for standing by me.......♥

Badada and Chotda you have always been my anchor, and as older siblings I adore you, except for the fact that I cant stand you both for more than an hour......♥

I owe this book to me and my foolishness.....

Preface

The first memory of me as me is of a five-year-old. My mother had made an elaborate head gear to protect my thick, long, curly hair on Holi. And I accompanied my two brothers outside. A young boy from the other street playfully sprayed coloured water on my dress, I started to whimper, slowly my whimper changed to loud cry as if somebody had beaten me. My brothers embarrassed tried to silence me, but I wouldn't, my crying just did not stop and eventually my father picked me up and took me home. That was the end of Holi for me, since then I have never even made an effort to play. And every year with the advent of Holi, my anxiety would increase and my inside would start to scream. When I saw people's face plastered with colour my anxiety would increase, it was the same for all festivals. The crowd. The colour, the noise, even the smell overwhelmed me. Thinking back, I think I should have taken it as a sign, I am not sure what the sign was for, but definitely a sign.

Growing up with two older brothers was tough, I mean you cannot be a girl and behave like a girl. My brothers were rumbunctious, loud and naughty and were constantly fighting with each other as well as boys in the neighbourhood. They never thought that I was any different from them. So I had to be equally strong, faster, louder and most importantly demanding. I was not very well loved as my mannerisms, my walk, the way I talked nothing was ladylike as my mother once delicately put it. My mother's youngest sister had a daughter and she was loved by all as she was soft, quiet, walked softly, cried at the drop of a hat and I envied her. People called me names when I was growing up, they would in colloquial language call me horsey, boyish, tomboy, scraggly cat. In Odia these terms sounded worse. But though it hurt I would never cry or show my emotions to anyone. There were times when in school I would be picked up because I could never sit in one place, it was almost as if my feet had wheels. I would hop from one seat to another. I was the first to be punished even if I had not done anything. There were times when the teacher would forget that I was standing outside in the hot sun holding on to my ears, but I rarely complained about this to my parents. I am still not sure why.

I was sickly too as a child, when I was young, I used to have bouts of febrile convulsions. I was diagnosed with juvenile arthritis and I had to take Penicillin for almost 12 years, till I was 18. I used to faint often and once I remember my father telling me that I had to be revived as my heart had stopped beating and my pulse was weak. But I never felt pain. And my mother kept telling me that my pain threshold was quite high. And I believed it as I remember once I was wearing my school uniform and it had not been ironed. Thinking that I could iron it on my own, I slid the hot iron on me while I was wearing my clothes; my chest, abdomen was completely burnt and I had these hot bubbles on me. They were painful, but I did not tell my parents and went to school in that condition. Night when my mother was trying to help me change, she saw it and she started to cry, seeing her cry I started to cry. My father rushed and both of them just stared at me, and then gently put some ointment on me. That day I heard my father tell my mother that we need to keep a eye on Sarita as she can hurt herself. I was eight.

When I was a child, I did not feel great when anybody touched me or hugged me. I just like it when my mother or father hugged me. I used to feel strange when people touched me. It just felt weird, there were times when emotion exhausted me. For example, if I saw someone crying it would immediately trigger my anxiety. I would be overwhelmed and start to cry, but the only time I had feeling was when I was with children or animals. I adored both. I have been bitten by dogs, puppies almost 30-40 times. And these bites did not deter me or stop me from grabbing them, hugging them, kissing them or bringing them home. I adored children, I never reacted when anyone hit me, or bit me or pinched me. Other than that, I did not have any friends. But it never mattered to me that I did not have any close friends. Anyone who was friends today would leave tomorrow. So, there was no expectation from people. I did not need any company, as I was perfectly fine with me. I climbed all the trees, rode my bicycle on my own, avoided my brothers like plague. And was constantly busy. I did have learning difficulties now when I think of, I realise. I was very bad in Mathematics. I just could not grasp the methods and my mind always went blank; I was poor and hated the period and also did not like the teachers teaching it. But I compensated it with a different way. I could absorb and remember and visualize everything that I read. So, I used that process to learn. I would remember the entire examples of the arithmetic chapter and whatever problem was given I would just write what I had picked up from the examples. I have never failed, but the way I handled mathematics probably helped me pass grades. Rest of the subjects were also treated the same way. But somehow, I was not bad and considered to be above average. And I managed to do well in college and university. But the funny thing is I still remember what I had studied during my childhood. I am not sure why and how have I managed to hold on remembering what I studied in each of the classes. I remember in third grade we had a chapter on, 'Shakuntala". The assignment was that we were supposed to recite the story the next day. I remember when I sat down to study, after an hour or so I was overwhelmed with anxiety and started to cry as I could not remember anything that I read, my breakdown was such that my mother forced me to go to bed. The next day I dreaded going to school, but when my turn came I without a pause narrated the whole story. It was a surprise for me. I surprised myself with my ability, and when I would read thoroughly and try to repeat it, my mind would go blank. These sporadic memory lapses used to surprise my parents. And every report card of mine would carry the comment, 'talkative and constantly distracted, would do better if she was careful and listened to the teachers. It was a joke in our family, and my brothers and parents would constantly tease me. My mood swings, my constant need to self harm and my dark mood swings, my angry out burst all had a reason and I did not know what the reason was. My thoughts were put into words and took the semblence of poems during those challenging hours, days, which could never be managed as I did not know why I was what i was.

The reason all of this comes to my mind is because now at the age of 56 I was diagnosed with ADHD and Bipolar Disorder. I remember when my doctor at VIMHANS, Delhi said this, I was stunned. I felt relief for the fact that at least now I know what it is, but I also felt saddened that I had lost so much as it was not diagnosed early. While growing up either people around me made fun of me or put me in a slot of not being like other girls, of running around like a mad woman, of not conforming to the rules set, and of being different. I so desperately wanted to fit in. my parents who were doctors in the most prestigious medical college also were treating most of my symptoms like burns as I had thrown myself on fire, fracture as i threw myself from the two wheeler not knowing why i was doing that,, my constant temper tantrums, my not understanding sometimes simple rules, they probably would have looked at it closely if during that time there was a deeper understanding on how to handle neurodivergent children.   Today I do hope somebody reads my poems and understands that i lived because I love life, irrespective of the darkness of mental health that I faced........

Acknowledgements

Thank you Bijoy, Naisha and Naima, I appreciate you all for standing by, bearing with my mood swings, caring for me during my most painful moment and not judging me during my illness. To all the feline and canine babies that I have had and still do have, because of you I have survived. My love to all twenty of you.

I love the fact that you have accepted me for who I am. I am ADHD and Bipolar, and I rock....

1 . That Deep Depression on Valentine's Day

That deep depression on Valentine's day,

The depression does not manipulate me to take my life, nor does it make me want to cry;

But it however pushes me to think and rethink;

How does one make relationship work? and how does one carry the weight of friendship to a natural culmination of sustained friendship, shared love, and swapping of stories and laughter till the end of life?

NO answers, NO suggestions,

Just a thought that I will probably carry to my grave, as there is no chance that I will change, and think about me first before I think of others.

Happy Valentine's Day...

2. Leave

I am yet to walk out of the dark dinghy house I call
home since ages.

i am yet to feel the warmth of the suns rays since ages.
The darkness is welcome, and I have been drowning in
this darkness, it soothes my skin and lets me wallow in
it.

The possibility of leading a live is futile unless I create an
utopia for myself

but....
utopia is a mere dream and I am not a dreamer.

3. Dancing Queen

She dances, her hands gracefully sway to the music,
Her desperation to be happy visible from the urgent
steps she takes.

She lashes out at life,
her dance unique, awe-inspiring and bold.

Refusing to take what life has to offer, her energy returns
 and she sways not only to the music but also to the pain
of life.

4. The Dream

I lie, I cheat, I hide my insanity,
hoping against hope that it will not be recognised as my
life unfolds like a comic strip.

I am the voice of insanity,
yet I am insanely sane, yet to be identified and put in a
compartment;
yet to be driven away from life and from the darkness
surrounding it.

I wait in hope to see and feel what others perceive is life.

5. Deep Sea

The play of life and the fact that death looms over all of us never ceases to surprise me.

Still we live life thinking that immortality is a step away.

If this is the truth, then does it matter that I am in a space of nothingness.
The space though boring seems safe, it prevents the pain from spreading; and my heart
which is dark and deep and carries layers and layers of pain seems protected in this maroon of nothingness.

6. Voices

I am a voice not necessarily the voice of reason.

My emotions play with my voice to such an extent that the tone and pitch sounds bizarre to me.

But then I see the faces of people listening to me, I realise that they still have not realised the tsunami of emotions playing within me.

The voices in my mind threatens to expose me. Wondering if exposed will I also have the same fate as the witches of Salem?

7. The Oasis of Life

A Deep overwhelming sadness I can't seem to get over it.

Why do they say memories fade away when you still remember the words that cut, the innuendos, the feel on the skin of the physical obscene touch?

I have walked the tragic path of pain and abuse, though it has been a while since, but festering wound just does not heal.

The pain seeps through the wound and spreads over the body and across my soul.

I do welcome the pain as I am sure it is a part of my healing process and a part of my life.

8. Heat and Dust

The dull dry heat along with the sand seeps through the pores of the skin.

Sunburnt, the skin toughened by years of toiling under the hot tropical sun.

Yet, not a word escapes her dry parched mouth.

She opens her legs wide and drops the tiny weak life, others catch it before it falls on the ground.

Unalive but her heart beats faintly; the parched dry lips ask, 'will she live?'

9. The river of life

The chill in the life takes my breath away.
I dared myself to jump into the deep cold river of life.

It chilled me till my soul and took my breath away.
It seems the darkest days are here, the saddest nights
have reached me.

What more can happen , how bad can life be for me?

10. The cracked heart

How do I stop my heart from crying;
There is no balm to reduce the intense pain;
Tried crying copious tears,
Walked the hell and scraped the sole of my feet; yet my
heart does not stop from crying.
Partied and opened my legs to reduce the pain in my
heart,
The diversion of pain that I sought did not take place,
and the pain would not stop.
I know my actions will eventually harden my heart, but
as of now am savouring the pain that a cracked heart
gives.

11. Will not go anywhere

I am not going anywhere once I die, so will savour every moment of my life till I live.
I am not going to love once I die, so will learn to love more and more till I live.
My hands will clasp other hands and learn how to walk with others till I live as I know I ain't going nowhere once I die.
I will smile, love and make peace with each and all as I know I am going nowhere once I leave.
I will savour every morning light and twinkle with the stars at night as I am not going to live forever and I ain't going nowhere once I die.

12. First Love

I was seven and was deep in my sleep when I awoke and saw a tall lady in blue.

She was a vision and so beautiful that I could not take of my eyes from her,

My dad gently knocked my head and said that is your Ma, can you not recognise her?

For a child of seven, this was a love that filled her heart and her smile, a smile so awesome and brilliant that it warmed her heart.

I am so happy, I feel wanted.
Immortal as I feel needed.

13. Mother

Learnt at the age of seven that ma was god...
she could do anything and my tears instantly would
turn into pearls.

Oh she was god as I have seen the halo on her head
shine brightly like a diamond, could never tell her how
magical it was living with her.

My fingers could trace the lines on her face, these lines
spoke back to me and this always brought back a smile
on mine and my siblings face.

..... and then one fine day she disappeared, since then I
knew she was god as after she left there was never a day
when my tears were wiped, nor where my hurts covered
with balms.

I realised that my god was no more.

14. Twists and Turns

Sometimes you have so many people around you that
you cannot breathe, you crave for solitude;
Sometimes you are completely alone craving for
company, and there is no one besides you.

Life is crazy that way, when you have more you want
less, when you have less you want more.

Life is funny too, when it is summer, you want winter,
And when it is winter you crave for summer.

Satisfaction towards what you have, what you do, how
you live; and balance between 'needs' and 'want' is the
core essence of life. But then

it is difficult to understand when you are young, but by
the time you comprehend it is late, you are left with
regrets on what you should have done, and how you
should have dealt with life.

15. Today

Wonderful day
filled with friendship and laughter,
sharing stories.
coming together and holding hands forever
Life has come to a full circle,
laughing at life
yelling at the inner as well as outer demons.
Friendship wins, Friendship lives.
Hope we continue to cherish this relationship,
together and towards the challenges of life.
Love you Gals!
May we have more of these wonderful days, friendship
and laughter.

16. The Cycle of Life

The cycle of life hides the episodes of violence and abuse that you see and you face.

But then, does this change the way you look at life ? Yes of course it does.

One does not take to drugs as is often thought of, though it could be an excuse for some to take drugs. But when one does they are shamed as self abuser's.

You feel as if there is nobody more uglier than you, you tend to avoid looking at the mirror, you often eat and distort your own image, more importantly your loss of self esteem ensures that you constantly put yourself down.

Life does not give you answers to what you go through, you need to seek answers as to whether you would like to continue in that self destructive mode or would switch to the sunny, optimistic bright human being you can be and you should be, the choice is yours"...............................

17. NIGHT AND DAY

The strength of the night is the fact that it hides the
secret and the dirt of the day;
At night you remember your past, folded into the pleats
of your memories,
you struggle to remember the colour of those memories
and the impact it left on your life and your desires.

Why does the night seem more friendly than the day?
 Is it because the stories of the night remain hidden
behind the shadows of darkness, or is it because the
stories though voyeurism has consequences.

The strength of the day is the fact that nothing remains
hidden anymore, the dirt, animosity, ugliness is open and
visible;

As the day progresses, one is dazzled by the colours that
one can see, the colours seems to merge and the eyes
closes by itself in pain looking at the vibrant yet harsh
colour which gives no joy to one's eyesight.

The play of the day and night makes it important to

recognise the fact that each moment gives its own desired performance; the comedy, tragedy, the excitement and the anticipation of the next moment makes it all the more important to survive another night and another day.

18. The Death of a Soul.

Today was a dark day, it was my birthday I lost a year to life and my soul too died.

I always thought that when my soul would die it would go with a blast and a bang.

But mine went with a fizzle. My energy died, my love for my family members died. Life for me will no longer be the same. I know now I am going to live waiting for my death.

Funny thing tears now don't fall as fast as it did. I am ready to die. Now I am not scared of death.

19. The New Me....

I am a reminder to you,
I prick your conscience and make you insecure,
I am what I am and cannot help it.

Take it or leave it,
but do not torment me with your forced indifference and
snide remarks
It makes me mad, and that is not a good feeling

20. Just a Thought

I woke up to a different universe today,

I mean it was still a sexist, racist, casteist world, with full
of hatred and was a place where people, responded with
violence, abuse and intolerance to anything that was
different and unique.

Though the conscience and the soul are an integral part
of the whole, yet it was divisive and full of hatred.
It seemed as if the universe had lost its soul.

But then along with this hatred was also the emergence
of soft voices of dissent which stood up to fight and
conquer.

With great humility I realised that this was what one
should do, stand firm, and stick to what is right, and give
the voice of truth a space to resonate for others to join.

21. None of us are going to Heaven

None of us are going to heaven;
The lies, deceit, and the savage brutality perpetrated by
us by our acts, actions and words,
None of us are going to heaven.

The passive acceptance of killing, the brutality in the
name of god, the anger, hatred in our heart does whisper
to us loudly that none of us will go to heaven.

While alive everything bothered us, the colour of skin,
the shape of the nose, the way we dressed, the size of our
curls; and the scarf on our head

Rejecting the universe lovingly built, rejected, mutiliated,
shredded piece by piece, slow by slow, hating it, berating
it, digging it, exploiting it, it took us very little time to
destroy it. So just remember none of us are going to
heaven.

And now waiting for the pearl gates to open, thinking
that it will open justifying all our actions as part of
living, but deep down one knows, a heinous act is an
insult to humanity,

So none of us will go to heaven.

23

22. Meandering Love

I keep falling in and out of love.

Each time I say no more, can't bear the pain that my heart goes through, but then I see a spark and run towards it again, only to be tormented and my life in chaos again.

The heart just does not stop trusting and seeking love.

I seem to have been putting my heart, lock stock and barrel, into the hands of others, trusting empty and loveless hearts,

I break my heart only to rise from the ashes of dead love to fall in love again;

I know I will keep doing that and keep searching for that perfect soul who will understand me and cherish me.

9 789369 542710